The Silence
Of
My Mind

Breska Liotson

To G. K. R. Crawford.

To Jaxsie, for all your support.

For Sae.

CONTENTS

The Silence
Of
My Mind

The Silence of My Mind

These Words are the Silence of my mind
      The clank of the gears, the click of the grind.
These Letters are a reflection of my Soul,
      The crack in the mirror that makes me whole.

This pen is a sword within my hand—
      Always more honest than ever I planned.
This ink is a blot within my heart,
      Never removed, always a part.

Those Lines are the images flickering by,
      Illusion of truth within the eye.
Those Phrases are pieces of paintings within,
      The Master's work of which I am kin.

That book is a map to guide my way,
      A broken Needle that leads me astray.
That page is a question defining me,
      The final response to setting me free.

Numbered Poetry

1

It disturbs me to find my future
Drifting before my nose
If I inhale it I might absorb it
Destroying all hope of attaining it
In passion I might breathe out
Pushing possibility away
For the future has already happened
But I have missed it in my own way
Still I continue to watch it
Holding my breath all the time
Revealing nothing but watching
And forgetting about losing time

2

I have a loneliness in me
I learnt it when I was young
Hiding below the counter
Amongst the pots and pans
I find my loneliness comforting
In its inescapable friendship
It goes with me always
Breaking the curse of breathing
To inhale is to feel it
But breathing is a necessity
So I stay reciprocal to social
And find my way through the deep
For no one can touch my loneliness
No soul's finger reaches in me
And break from life I must
And break from this world I will
For I have a loneliness in me

3

What I wondered
In the first hour of morning
Staring at the gray ceiling
Is what is the Other thinking
In the bowels of that broken mind
Does the Other even think
Or does that one just speak
Forgetting the other convention
Of reason before realization
Or does the Other forget
That life exists at all
And thinking is no longer needed
Without the truth of life
I'd bet the Other forgot
But would I ever forget
Staring at the gray ceiling
In the first hour of morning
I quietly wondered

4

I forgot to bring my brain
To class with me that day
I didn't know I could remove it
Much less throw it away
Did God go through this insanity
On Earth in Hebrew school
I'll bet he was a perfect student
For dissention way too cool
But that is God and not me
For I am never that good
Leaving my brain in the closet
Instead of my cranial hood
Ironically I didn't need it
You don't need to think to agree
So no one noticed the empty skull
No question tormented me

5

Light and sound are all you need
To imitate the evidence of life
And funny how a polyester strip
Can hold both pieces at bay
And that I can move this image
I hold the semblance of life
My waiting hands forgive not
The helpless imitation
For I know it is hopeless
If a light and a sound can create
An imitation of life
Enough to fool the eye
Enough for you to believe

6

Love is a curse upon the soul
Barring reason from the mind
And forcing fear to invade
Without this terrible convention
I would not be alive
So does that make it a good curse
Or is it a curse no matter

7

Little boxes
They surround me
Making bricks
Boxing me in
Without my world
It's a folly
Gone with peace
Gone with day
Without the light
Without the truth
I find my boxes
Closing in
Forget the bound'ry
Forget the soul
It's life I seek
And dying's day
Though I can see
The painful unit
Brushing death
And holding me
I never leave
These little boxes
Staying with
This endless day

8

Echoing my soul's first longing
I met life with holder's fear
In power's distance I abhor this
Echoed truth in artist's day
Forgetting life's forgotten truth
Without the echo of this light
I find a power in the night cap
Laying down my soul to sleep
I walk away as truth approaches
Framing fear upon my brow
Did life rehash my painful anguish
Recollecting truth today
Am I alone in all my yearning
Am I to stand before the day
Or will my heart forget my silence
As I release my pain-filled fear

9

I have died from a billion lifetimes
Lives I barely know now
I remember the murders and the shame
And the death in life's old age
But still I continue to live
New lives still come my way
It seems I have yet to learn
What life's existence is for
Without this impassioned debate
Would I continue to allow myself birth
Or would I quietly stop
And fade swiftly away

10

Why is everybody everywhere
And I am stuck here
In my head
In my thoughts
While they travel the world to their heart's content
Why is everybody everywhere
And I am stuck here
Stuck without the means to be everywhere
Stuck without the drive to be everywhere
If I go everywhere I could lose everything
I could lose my security
My safety
My mind eventually
But still
Why is everybody everywhere
And I am stuck here

11

Where am I?
Am I where you are too?
Sitting and waiting for something to happen
Sitting and waiting for things to start
Living in this waiting room of life
For dreams to come get me
And fantasy to be reality
But where am I really?
At a desk in a sad office?
Orange walls to color my backgrounds?
Or in a school with so many classes ahead?
Or just here, where I usually am, in a parking lot waiting?
Always waiting
Like a rock in a river with the water rushing by
Feeling like *life* is rushing by
Or others are sailing past on life
But I don't know
Where am I?
Am I where you are too?

12

I imagine things happening
Just like me
They don't
And aren't real
Just like me
Imagine or hallucinate
What's the difference
What's the truth
But just like me
They don't
Know the truth
Exist
I imagine things happening
Just like me
That aren't real
And don't exist

13

Apart or a part
The whole for the division
The space for the singular
The implication of a split
In the whole piece
The world breaking
The piece coming together
One or more than one
The words reversing inherent meaning
The visual not representative of meaning
But broken
Apart or a part

Fragments

Wicked are the hours
In which I wait,
For one suggestion
Of your soul near mine;
I cannot abide
These lonely spaces,
The coldness coming close
And warming me.

Electric are the points
That contact me,
Blue is the light
That hums and breaks the Lee;
This lonely moment
Exhales its stolid light,
Refines the touch
And heals the heart of blight.

Love

A faint hand at my throat,
Constricts the airway of my life,
And I cannot withstand it more,
And I cannot love him less.

I wish he would just hate me,
So I could forget I love him,
And let go of perfection,
And let go—

Smooth water runs by rocks by day,
And the rocks never shift aside;
They stand still, waiting for a leaf—
Pushed by the water to pass again.

A single edge of a dying leaf,
Changes the surface not at all,
But once the touch is felt,
It cannot be easily forgotten.

Fresh is the air I breathe
Kind is the Time,
When you are close and me
Not far behind;
And yet I have not redeemed
This one embrace,
To change the here and now,
To change this space.

———————————————————————————

Where did you go—
      Now that you're gone
Have you really left—
      Or am I not here

A quiet space for
Entertainment
Giggles and thrills
Gasps and chills
Illusion as reality
Sometimes in 3D

Scores of silence
Notes of notice
Chords of chaos
Echoes of etherealism

Set the stage for your ears
Set the tone for film gears

Why bother with self improvement
When my self sabotage
Will always be stronger

Worthless
Everything I do is worthless
Because when I do it
It is suddenly somehow
Worth *less*

Riddle

A feeling, an instinct,
A sense of disgust
An unacceptable thing
A large amount of something
A quantity before net
A dozen dozen
An income

Repress it
always repress it
No one wants to see that
or deal with that
        or fix that
No one cares enough to try
Repress it

If you knew the day you'd die
      Would you continue that same path?
Would you walk? Would you talk?
      Would you let yourself feel wrath?

I look around and I am sad
But sad of *what?*
And is it sad too?

And darkness fell
And Sunset on that Day
There is no Dawn here
No hope to yield
No heart to sway

Will you ever lose yourself
the way I have lost me?
Are you stable inside?

There are strangers
closer than us, but
we are

close

in other ways.

The day is at an end;
My life is at its close;
I've chosen to take a path
I will never fully know.

Should I ever reach my home,
When I see it will I know
That this home is the only place
I have ever chosen to go.

Other Poetry

Pilgrim Soldier, Abandon Sailor

Nobody ever goes home anymore,
Not since the call of the brave.
They left for the sea-beaten shore,
And a new world where men won't behave.

No one ever returns home,
From the lives they've chosen to live.
Lost on the paths they now roam,
Their souls have nothing to give.

Nobody ever gets home inside,
While running from their only hope.
Away from all reason their hearts often hide,
As they let go the anchor rope.

No one ever goes home again,
To the innocence childhood stole.
You cannot regain where you've been,
As a horse cannot be a foal.

Almost

If Almost is meaningless in the war of love,
Then maybe this love is meaningless too.
      For I love you but Almost is where we will stay,
      I love you but Almost is where we will be.

And what about "could be" in this Chess match?
What about what *could* still happen?
      It's never conditionals that decide the game,
      It's never conditionals that win.

And if nothing happens—today or ever—
Will I still feel the pain in the morrow?
Will love still hold me, will this passion last?
      Or will I have *forgotten* by next week's end?

I know not where we stand, nor do I care,
I only care that my heart hurts.
      And yet in this paradox, with my mind unhinged
      I do not know—and I seek to know.

For if I could love you, freely and truly,
      I am afraid that it would never last,
      I am afraid that my fickle heart would stop,
      I am afraid that my attention would *w a n d e r*.

So perhaps it is best, this Almost world,
The way we skirt each other endlessly;
      For I love you too much to burn you that way,
      And I know I would, in the end.

Horizon

Dawn breaks upon the shoreline—
Is it dawn, or is it day?—
My life and heart entwine now,
And my tears are brushed away.

What fire controls my heart?
I cannot tell, nor wish to say;
What whispers I attend to,
Whisper on through night and day.

I left someone behind now—
In the surf *(please let me stay!)*.
I've lost most of myself here,
Found another in the fray.

Memory will not fail me,
Nor will my sense of dawn and day;
As new dawn breaks for them (and me),
Walk your path: don't go astray.

Honestly

What would I do if heart were torn?
        If child were lost before it's born?
        If friend was taken at their time?
        If heart repeated broken rhyme?

If these were lost and soon forsaken,
        I'd feel the worth of life mistaken.
For in each breath lies hope for all,
        Hope that hope will never fall.

And what if our blind trust does fail?
        Will we trip in our steps and let go the rail?
        Will we fail our friends and change our stride?
        Will we take our revenge on all who's lied?

As we look and find our true selves' face, —
        (And find the ideal mask to replace) —
The image engraved upon my soul,
        Has never been hope's lonely goal.

Theater 2

There is a stillness in the air
There is a silence in this room
Now that the day is over
Now that the show is done

The light is almost gone now
The theater quiet at last
The buzz of the last scene is silent
The hum of the movie is deafened

The walls remember what I see
The seats feel it as well
At dawn when the room reawakens
The story rebirths into life

For now the room is silent
Here, where even hearts won't beat
Each moment moves me forward
Each breath infuses my soul

My reason for perpetual return

Our/Hour

If I had an hour
It would not be enough
To capture the peace I feel:
Here in a theater
Where I am alone,
Here in the theater
With only me.
If I had an hour
To tell the truth
It would not be long enough still:
To tell you things from in my past,
The things
This theater
Just knows.
If I had an hour
(Perhaps my last)
I would spend it
Right in this seat:
Where I feel at home,
Alone
At night
While the theaters
Breathe out
The day's work.
If I had an hour
Or maybe six more
I'd spend it right here
With you:
To tell you these things
In my hidden worlds,
Till you see me
Like I see you.
If I had an hour—

But I don't,
Do I?—
To spend or save
In this room:
I'd keep it here
Deep within
Waiting for time to pass.

Waiting

An hour or more of silence
A racing, uninterpreting mind
The heartbeat settling for the night
I succumb to darkness's might
For all that is left is the waiting
All that is left is the mind
And I wash away my sorrow
My soul waits for tomorrow
For traveling swift my heart breaks
But I still have some time
I wait for light to touch me
Tonight I will drown in the sea

Birth/Death

I could never choose to take that final walk,
To graven images soon quickly stalk,
And walk between the frozen letter-lines:
An epitaph which to life now glaring shines.

Perhaps I'll go to grave-dance There someday,
I hope the Journey wanders a twisting way,
And that the Place waiting soon behind—
Is all that was imagined by poet's mind.

They say birth is the death of the dead,
And death should not be met with dread,
To take this advice I have not been inclined,
To walk to the grave straight-backed and refined.

It's in this thought that one will find what's true:
That birth is just the change from old to new,
That birth is what changed death into life,
And credit's due to birth: Creator of Strife.

There will be no great sentence upon my grave,
None like, "She fought a battle, lost, but she was brave."
I may not have won a battle—yet or at all,
But into my grave, before my time, I will not fall.

Remembered Me

There was a girl who resembled me:
Same hair, same skin,
same need to be free.
How did she deviate from the form of me?
The tattered and shorn robe,
the scars this girl's known.
A past has caught up, her weaknesses
found.
Her attacker's revealed
from a face she'd once known.
So what happened to the girl
who resembled me?
I've looked for her recently
and found one thing
about this girl who resembled me;
(same hair, same skin,
same need to be free).
Her skin is my skin,
her scars are on me;
my hair is cut short, but
it's her hair I see;
my clothes are her clothes,
my favorite shirt hers;
And the scars and the past,
And the attacker she's known
Are all that's left,
Are all that I own.

Depression

There is a sadness in me
It grew here when I was young
Every year it grows with me
A testament to pain unsung

The sadness burrows deep in my soul
A fragment of my former self
Stealing the echoes of youth's hope
And taking other feelings I've felt

In the dark the sadness seems bigger
A monstrous growing beast
Lurking and stalking and stealing
Just waiting to kill me again

I'm a stranger to myself now
The sadness has stolen my face
Every shred left is a farce
A demon pretending to be me

Any beacon of light offers escape
I shunned these for the blanket of dark
Here I know the pain
The light brings new pain and new tears

So I sink again into darkness
Let the sadness take all of me
Shrouding my real self deep within
Pretending to be me though I'm gone

Impoverished

The image in my mind of poverty
Does not ever include an image of me
So jarring is the thought inside my mind
Impoverished is who I am, what I find

Emaciation marks the poverty line
But poverty is never far from you or me
Dancing nearby, laughing at your plight
Till you find yourself slinking in the night

Morning Rush

Tick tock
Coffee shop
Caffeinate
Wait I'm late

Tick tock
Broken clock
Daily grind
Lost my mind

Tick tock
Work won't stop
What's the deal
No free meal

Ledge

Voices in my head
Yelling screaming voices
telling me I'm not—
good enough
nice enough
smart enough
any enough
Screaming at me to
shut up
go home
you're stupid
YOU'RE STUPID
just stop
Because I'm not enough
I'm never enough
Enough for my depression
my fear
my trauma
my mental health
Enough to beat them
cope with them
overcome them
Memes lie
Positivism lies
The voices are always there
telling me to quit and
DIE
and sometimes I listen
Sometimes I make a plan
Sometimes I fear
who I am
Some days are better
Some days are not

Everyday is a gamble
whether I find myself
out on a
ledge
breathing and looking down
or blinking and turning around
But I don't know
and I wake up uncertain
most days
whether the voices are silent
or LOUD
and whether or not
I am here

Alone

Let me talk to an octopus for a day
To understand that curly-cue mind
And perhaps in mind a soul
A soul unlike mine
But let me talk to one—
No not to speak
to understand
and hear what they think
What must it be like to see as they do
in oceans
in tidepools
in light and in dark
on rainbow reefs and shallow places
skimming over surfaces at the bottom of all things
Still I long to know what they know
see what they see
and know what I know to be true—
That perhaps they *do* think
and are people like us
dreaming and scheming
living their feisty ways
Or perhaps I just hope for that
hope that we as humans
are not alone in our thoughts after all
that the octopus
thinks
with us
too

Hollow places

All of these hollowed out places
And all of the hollowed out faces
Filled with despair and displacement
Their lives gone from security to wasteland
Burned out homes and empty churches
Fallen in roofs and crumbling walls
Their souls long for reprieve
Their anger gone quiet
Despair has silenced their cries
Where is the factory now?
Where is the once-was livelihood?
Where is the fight and the faith?
Gone like the Bessemer process
Gone like the security of old
Gone like the heart of the town
Gone when no one was watching
These left-behind people wait for hope
Their grit keeps them living and looking
Any voice speaking lies gives them hope
Because that voice speaks to them at long last
But where is true hope for the lost?
And then will these hollowed out places be whole?

NOT nice

I'm not a nice person anymore
Trauma has chased the nice out
And I am angry in my pain
Why is it a virtue to be kind
In the face of trauma?
As if the anger is unwarranted
And out of place
Or wrong somehow
But maybe anger is the right response
And not being a nice person
Is actually how I should be
Angry and filled with pain
Letting myself spew vitriol
Because maybe that is the way to heal
To acknowledge the anger
Rather than repress it

Abate

Sitting alone in a Walmart parking lot
Eating McDonald's
Listening to music
Waiting for the loneliness to abate
And the desire to be a person to return
But I don't feel like being a person
I feel like sitting here alone
Ignoring the day's tasks
Ignoring productivity
Ignoring even me
As I sit alone
In a Walmart parking lot
Eating McDonald's
And wait

Crossing

At night I hear the train sound
Passing in the yard nearby
A symphony of steel and structure
A mile of metal on the fly

My mind wanders quiet in the dark
Drifting after that barreling train
Pondering the places it roams
Taking the track off the main

I tumble along that steele course
It's symphony felt deep within
Luring me out of my dark room
To places it's already been

Then the silence falls
And I fall back into bed
The train may have traveled through town
But its horn haunts the halls of my head

Lasting

Lingering loathing in the mind
Poisoning heart and poisoning lie
Fighting for top voice in the eye
Abhorring absorbing remaining sight
Preventing forgiveness from settling in
Last best effort of avoiding the grim
Fighting for stopping and forging for trust
With mind in heart consumed with fire
Never yielding to lasting love
Where flame once stood only coldness remains
This lingering loathing changing the game

The Balance

How do we know which way to go
Which life do we choose if we even can
Does desire override need
Does desire override right
Do we even know what's right
while desire cripples that sight
Does life endure through choices' changes
How do we accept those changes
Especially if we don't really choose
        or if we choose at all

A winter evening at home

The chill in the air
And in the night
The sun is gone and has taken the light

The grey in the clouds
Sky laden down
Not a flake to be seen, none on the ground

The blanket on my bed
Silence in my head
I sleep in comfort, my soul is fed

Unheard

My heart is broken
My soul, a piece stolen
I find myself alone at last
Bending to the will of the past

My heart hears silence
My cries go unheard
Am I alone? Is anyone here?
Will I drown in this sea of tears?

Does it matter?

Will I leave of my own accord
And find my way again?

Tough

You're miserable? You're sad?
You have it bad and you are mad?
Tough.
Others have it worse. Others deal with worse.
Others are alone or homeless or broken.
Tough.
You don't have enough to deal with to complain.
You don't have enough to beg for relief.
Tough.
The world broke you? The world bend your soul?
Others have it worse so—
TOUGH.

Hustle to fix your finances.
Are you making money from your hobbies?
You're not allowed to just love a thing, you have to own that thing
        too.
You don't want to?
TOUGH.

Is it fair to say your suffering is not valid? Just because others have it
        worse?
Does the world have a right to decide which suffering is valid?
You don't think so?
TOUGH.

Will Always

Whatever you think
Whatever you see
Your life will always matter to me

Your voice in my mind
Your words in my heart
Your presence will always matter to me

After decades of love
After decades of truth
Your soul will always matter to me

Sentiment and romance
And friendship and kindness
You will always matter to me

Sonnets

Constrained to sentences prescribed
By eyes of masters from the past
In sentences their work described
And time delayed and made it last;
Setting rhymes in certain schemes
And cadences to certain meters
Perhaps confined to certain themes
Perhaps because they thought it neater.
Modern masters break the mold
Defying standards set before
And letting go of forms of old
To write the message at the core.
And yet some masters do go back
To forms their current work can lack.

You are the light in all these corner spaces,
Where Darkness seemed to be the only way,
And time does not slow down nor life replaces
Shivering shadow with the break of day.
And yet in your bright streams I am undone
Feeling the power and passion running free,
So that the fetters set in ashen sun
Could on this day break once and let me be.
Is it your light is strong or bonds are slight
That one brief moment wept and caved to truth,
Or is it I prefer your golden light
To folly I committed in my youth?
Perhaps I know the reason for this bliss:
That Love draws me to you, that Love is *this*.

For golden stream of fading setting Sun,
For light in eyes and pushing past behind,
For all the games I thought had long been done,
And all the echoes racing through my mind.
I read a sign, or cross the street, before—
Before I lose the chance to speak again;
I choke a greeting but can say no more,
Or speak of all the places I have been.
Yet in my heart you walked the same gray road,
And with my guiding sight you saw through me,
So in a sense you walked a path I owed—
You for the times I thought it best to flee.
And so I walk and let the light shine through;
I found my path, my way, and I found you.

Mistakes I've made I cannot ever count,
But on I move through tears and breaking down,
So that I look within and then surmount,
The violent truth still lurking below the crown.
Can I face the mirror's sharp cutting truth?
Do I know the mirage now judging me?
Or is this look a hidden broken youth?
Complete with folly and paths I didn't see?
I chose to be naïve without remorse,
Made choices imposed by my beating heart,
Did I once choose the improbable course?
The path I don't regret but chose to part?
And will I ever face this vacant space?
The soulless, callous actions from which I race?

Him, he who plagues my broken eyes and mind,
Who forced me from his life—or I forced me,
And all the choices left in bitter blind—
Where oft I looked again and didn't see.
He, the other him who haunts me still,
The past, the shadow, the façade of light,
Illusion threatening me and my will,
The coercer whose choice I did not fight.
And they, the two, the big ones overwhelmed—
The past, the one with conventional shame,
The present on which Hope's heart's path is helmed—
By choice—but are they really one and same?
And I forget all else when in one's space:
And I as me cannot—not one—erase.

Hard truths abound and threaten me,
My voice in silence cries out in reprimand,
And still in silence I refuse to see,
That all the things I forgot I forget to demand.
How can I act without a choice?
Can I choose without choosing's mind?
And speak in silence without audible voice?
So that the life I live I cannot even find?
I acted without grace or kindness then,
I chose to choose my dark side, rejected light,
And yet I think I'd make the choice again,
Though with this choice comes harsh and real hindsight.
Perhaps I could rethink my thinking's ways,
And live again to choose my better days.

Funny how choices start in small spaces,
And then our next decision grows a bit,
Until the choices fill the open places,
Where all our lives have grown and try to fit.
So that if in the past your mistakes were small,
And then you repeated them again and again,
The space grew wide, and long, and very tall,
And the mistakes grew to fill the spaces you had been.
Which means if in the past you didn't learn,
Or try to understand the lessons there,
Your newest space you never did once earn,
Or make reality lay itself out bare.
I still say this: I still say Hope exists—
That choices change and errors don't persist.

"I warned you"

Capture my flying, beating heart,
The rebellious organ that torments me,
Keep that still and unresisting part,
If you are the right one to set me free.
I cannot be restrained by Not-Love's hold,
But loyal I have been—and fiercely so—
Such that I can make those choices bold,
And jump impulsive into the places you go.
But if you aren't the right one for my life,
The right one who tries to capture this—
Quick! Cut this cord with laser-sharpened knife—
Release yourself! This never will be Bliss!
But if you are the one that God deemed right,
Then stay with me, ensnare me with your Light.

You are the one who created Fear in me!
Terror fills my veins with just one thought—
So how is this dark thing good to be?
Have I failed? Have I stumbled? Have I fought?
All thoughts of you petrify my soul,
I cannot escape this cornered-reality;
I find myself in darkness black as coal,
A child desperate, grasping fantasy.
You move—wind filling spaces where you were—
Try as I might to catch you in my hand—
You can't be caught—*just once!*—a moving blur!
You scare me! Don't you understand?
But no, I'm frozen to speak so you can't hear—
That your resisting presence gives me Fear!

I let my mem'ries fade into the waste,
Forgot the past and present's winking hold,
Gave up the chains for that one haunting taste,
And deafly heard convention's bitter scold.
Without the silence in your cloying eyes,
Without resistance to restrained desire,
To know I would not lose my present lies,
Surrender to the kiss of grasping fire.
Control slips down into the darkened night,
To eat away at fetters once held strong,
Yet I cannot feel conflict in this flight—
To action which convention would hold wrong.
And so I clutch with arms—also let go—
Giving away, conceding all control.

In Memoriam

I could be driving, gaze focused on road,
Or walking 'cross the quad where old are young,
Or maybe in my quickened daily mode,
On land where once your shining bell was rung.
At stop-light, or mid-step, my mind will pause,
A jarring discord in my living life,
And wait, I think, but never find the flaws,
Or find the cuts made deep by Death's long knife.
But still I know there is a missing void,
A kind unkindness, cut-out in my heart,
A vanished print like burning celluloid,
Lurking 'round the corner's counterpart.
But without stilled-bell's silence in my day,
I know your Memory would soon slink away.

I died a million deaths in Holy grace,
And still a million more by coldest kill;
I've died in times when death was one disgrace—
I could not find myself in broken quill.
I forged my sword from sunshine's hardest light,
Split blade in two and scattered 'round the world—
And hid the pieces in the darkest night,
Until the bleeding flag one day unfurled.
I waited in the dark outside of Life,
Awaiting judgment passed before my birth,
Only to wake in pain with hand on knife,
Seeing the truth and laughing without mirth.
And still my soul waits for resolution,
A last reprieve: Gift of Absolution.

The Fresh Start (COVID-19 edition)

What has come and what has gone
What has been held and then let go
What opened eyes did not then know
What world we face with each new dawn
What problems built from ocean away
What daily grind we took for granted
What isolation has supplanted
What stranger life we live today
What in this time we hold most dear
What family stranger and long lost friend
What digital contact on which we depend
What will not ever make us fear
What this new life will not suspend
What is not now is not the End

ABOUT THE AUTHOR

Breska Liotson is an incidental poet who stumbled into the artform at age eleven. Though her work has matured since then, she still looks back on those poems fondly as an early expression of some then-important topics.

She lives on the east coast.

www.ingramcontent.com/pod-product-compliance
Lightning Source LLC
Chambersburg PA
CBHW021139020426
42331CB00005B/832